THE

camp·ing
DICTIONARY

THE
camp•ing
DICTIONARY

Heather Balogh Rochfort

Workman Publishing • New York

Workman
Workman Publishing
Hachette Book Group, Inc.
1290 Avenue of the Americas
New York, NY 10104
workman.com

Workman is an imprint of Workman Publishing, a division
of Hachette Book Group, Inc. The Workman name and logo
are registered trademarks of Hachette Book Group, Inc.

Design by Rae Ann Spitzenberger and Reagan Ruff
Illustrations by Joe Dator

Workman books may be purchased in bulk for business,
educational, or promotional use. For information, please contact
your local bookseller or the Hachette Book Group Special
Markets Department at special.markets@hbgusa.com.

Library of Congress Cataloging-in-Publication Data is available.

ISBN 978-1-5235-2975-9 (paperback)
ISBN 978-1-5235-2976-6 (ebook)

First Edition March 2026

Printed in China (APS) on responsibly sourced paper.

Cover © 2026 Hachette Book Group, Inc.

10 9 8 7 6 5 4 3 2 1

To my daughter:
I promise you'll thank me for
these memories someday.

To my husband:
For your unwavering positivity in
the face of torrential rain, broken tent poles,
and that one time a mouse crawled into your
beard—you're the real wilderness MVP.

To my parents:
You took me camping.
I made it a job. I owe you.

A

adventure /əd-ˈven-chər/ *noun:* An unusual or exciting experience, or a voluntary hardship that you can chat about in your social circles for years to come. One person's camping adventure is another person's hell, so it's really a questionable word that's wigglier than a bowl of Jell-O.

A-frame /ˈā-ˌfrām/ *noun:* A type of triangular tent that defies all logic. A-frame roofs are quite cute (and somewhat functional) when they're plopped on a quaint cabin tucked beneath a leafy canopy of trees. In tent form, however, they're merely cute—end of thought. The triangular shape means that only one camper can realistically sleep inside; multiple campers can expect damp hair from the condensation and smashed heads from the sloped ceiling just about every time they sit upright.

air out /ˈer ˈau̇t/ *verb:* To allow your clothes and/or body to experience the joy of fresh air after hours of being trapped within their own trail funk.

alpine start /ˈal-ˌpīn ˈstärt/ **noun:** The time in the morning that is so awkwardly early even the roosters aren't yet awake. The term comes from the mountaineers who often wake up just past midnight to begin their ascents before sunlight hits the snowpack, rendering it unstable (and yes, they call this a good time). For mere mortals, an alpine start may be as late as 5 a.m.—just early enough to get you on the summit before afternoon storms roll in, but late enough that you can still enjoy a little stargazing from your tent when you go to bed at dinner time.

alpine zone /ˈal-ˌpīn ˈzōn/ *noun:* The part of a mountain where the altitude is so high that even trees can't grow there and mountain goats often reconsider their life choices. While there is no universal elevation to indicate when you've hit the alpine zone—it varies depending on the region—you'll know you've arrived once you morph into a lightning rod, as you're now the tallest thing around. You'll also be sucking wind like you just ran a marathon, even while sitting down.

altimeter /al-ˈti-mə-tər/ *noun:* **1.** A tiny, wrist-worn trail gadget that tells you how shockingly little progress you've made so far on your climb. **2.** A tech device used by Instagrammers who can't wait to post "5,000 feet of gain, baby!"

See also: GPS watch

alpine zone

Appalachian Trail (A.T.)

/ˌa-pə-ˈlā-ch(ē-)ən ˈtrāl/ *noun:* A 2,200-mile-long
hiking route stretching 14 states from Springer
Mountain, Georgia, to Mount Katahdin, Maine.
This popular camping superhighway is covered
with dispersed campsites, designated camping
areas, and various shelters for the more than
three million hikers who tackle sections or the
entire thing every year. Pro tip: If you're ever
unsure what you're doing with your life, the
A.T. has magical dirt that will help you solve
all of life's mysteries. And if things don't shake
out, at least you'll grow your glutes.

B

backcountry /ˈbak-ˌkən-trē/ *noun:* A

remote and isolated geographic region that is
completely devoid of humans and yet teems
with creepy crawlies and other wildlife that
might very well want to cohabitate with you in
that fancy nylon palace you brought. Hardcore
outdoorspeople wear the word *backcountry*
as a badge of honor in an effort to prove they
can hike farther and sleep in dirt longer than
those who choose the bougie comforts of a
campground.

backpack /'bak-ˌpak/ *noun:* **1.** A supposedly portable sack imbued with magical powers that make it feel heavier the farther you hike. **2.** A carrying device similar to Mary Poppins's mysterious carpet bag in its ability to swallow everything you need—and a lot of what you don't. For example, how in the world did that family-sized bar of chocolate get in there?

backpacking /ˈbak-ˌpa-kiŋ/ **_verb:_** The art of filling a polyester sack with all your worldly essentials, then carrying the soul-crushing weight on your shoulders and venturing an unknown distance into the wilderness where you'll surely be cold, have to sleep on the ground, and run into any number of furry carnivorous mammals. And when you wake up in the morning, aching and sore from toting your entire home using muscles that aren't meant to work that way, you'll get to pack everything up and haul it all over again.

base weight /ˈbās ˈwāt/ *noun:* The numerical value (often measured in ounces) of all your gear minus the consumables like food, water, and fuel. This term is only used by the rare species of backpacker who eschews all logic and rational thought and prefers to hike hundreds or even thousands of miles in one go. For this type, achieving a lower base weight is a competitive sport, often requiring drastic measures such as sawing a toothbrush in half or counting out squares of toilet paper.

See also: gram weenie

bear banger /ˈber ˈbaŋ-ər/ *noun:* A small, pen-like flare device that makes a banging sound louder than the mosh pit at a Rage Against the Machine concert. If you've ever wanted to test the durability of your ear drums, now is your chance. There's about a fifty-fifty chance it'll scare away the bear, if only because she'll wonder why the biped covered in GORE-TEX is attempting to stay atop the food chain by causing such a ridiculous ruckus.

See also: bearanoia

bear canister /ˈber ˈka-nə-stər/ *noun:* A portable locker designed for backpacking; also referred to as a bear vault. This awkwardly large cylindrical container is expected to somehow fit inside your backpack so you can stash all your smellies and delicious snacks in it without a bear sniffing your goods.

bear hang /'ber 'haŋ/ *noun:* **1.** A human-designed system where campers stuff a bag full of their tasty food, snacks, and stinky toiletries, then attach a rope to the bag and go full cowboy as they try to fling it over a tree branch to suspend the bag in the air. If you're good at it, you might get it right on the first throw; otherwise, plan on spending a solid 20 minutes working on your lasso skills. **2.** A human-designed system to make bears sit on the ground and stare mournfully at a lost meal. When hung improperly, however, a bear hang is a thoughtful way to consolidate all your food in one place so the bear can enjoy a delectable selection of dehydrated delicacies without expending too much energy.

bear locker /ˈber ˈlä-kər/ *noun:* A rugged, durable metal box designed to safely store food and toiletries away from wildlife in campgrounds. Despite what we were taught in kindergarten, in this instance, sharing is not caring.

bear spray /'ber 'sprā/ *noun:* A burning substance consisting mainly of capsaicin that hurts like the fire of a thousand suns if it infiltrates your sack of flesh through your delicate eyes, nose, or mouth. While designed specifically for use on bears at those times when playing dead feels like too much of a commitment, bear spray has been known to accidentally take out an errant human with bad aim. Capsaicin is also the ingredient that gives chili peppers heat, but please do not spray down your chili mac after forgetting to pack the hot sauce.

bearanoia /ˌber-ə-ˈnȯi-ə/ *noun:* That feeling at camp when you're certain that twelve grizzly bears are going to spring into your tent at any moment to dine on your carcass, eat all your s'mores fixings for dessert, and then take a snooze inside your cozy sleeping bag.

beaver fever /ˈbē-vər ˈfē-vər/ *noun:*

1. An absolute disaster of a slang term for the sickness brought on by giardia. **2.** Nature's way of confirming you made a terrible, horrible, no-good life choice by drinking unfiltered water. Stomach cramps, nausea, diarrhea, severe gas, and profound regret are all common symptoms.

See also: giardia, water filter

biner /'bē-nər/ *noun:* Shorthand for carabiner, the small metal device that heroically transforms even the most disorganized backpackers into bona fide trail warriors. No longer will you be restricted by the confines of your backpack's interior—with a biner, your carrying potential is limitless. Clip some Crocs here, a stuff sack of snacks there, or a trucker cap up top for good measure. Before you know it, the inside of your pack will be virtually useless.

See also: stuff sack

binoculars /bī-'nä-kyə-lərz/ *noun:* **1.** A pocket-sized creeper kit perfect for those times when you really need to spy on a mountain goat, black bear, or that suspicious neighbor two campsites over. **2.** An armchair explorer's best friend. Who needs to hit the trail when you can stay in the parking lot with a pair of binocs and a caramel macchiato?

bivouac /ˈbi-və-ˌwak/ *noun:* A temporary or minimalist camp setup in which campers forgo a tent or any other type of structure. ***verb:*** To literally sleep in the dirt. While bivouacking enjoys a reputation as an extreme form of camping for hardcore or ultralight campers only, it's really a cop-out for those who aren't willing to carry a few extra pounds of weight.

black water /ˈblak ˈwȯ-tər/ *noun:* Toilet

wastewater in RV campers and campgrounds. Whenever you head into your RV or trailer for your post-coffee morning routine, whatever you expel goes into a tank and mixes with all the other horrific bathroom juices to form black water. The name comes from the dark, murky coloring resulting from the questionable meals consumed around a campfire, but it's also the color of your soul after your initial attempt to drain the black water tank. Unfortunately, no one does this correctly the first time. And, yes, that is poop on your shoes.

See also: dump station

bladder /ˈbla-dər/ *noun:* A malleable plastic pouch, much like the most annoying organ in our body, designed to hold water inside your hiking backpack. Also known as a water reservoir or hydration bladder, it is typically attached to a long tube that wraps over your shoulder so you can sip while trekking. Bladders can be incredibly useful not only for hydrating on the move, but also for leaking water into your backpack when you least expect it and for defying all logic in the science of mold growth. If you've always wanted to witness the expansion of rapid-spread green fur somewhere other than a petri dish, here's your chance.

blaze /'blāz/ *noun:* **1.** A painted or carved trail marker that assures hikers they are not yet lost. **2.** Google Maps, but for nature.

blister sister /'bli-stər 'si-stər/ *noun:* A loyal trail companion who stays with you, if only so you can remind each other that you both need better hiking socks.

See also: trail family

body wipe /ˈbä-dē ˈwīp/ *noun:* A wet swatch of fabric that's the closest thing to a shower after a week in the backcountry. Often applied with a questionable sense of optimism that you will technically smell better now.

boondocking /ˈbün-ˌdä-kiŋ/ *verb:* RV or trailer camping for free on public lands; also known as dry camping. The practice is similar to backpacking in that boondockers have perfected the art of sleeping in the middle of nowhere without relying on hookups, civilization, or amenities—aside from the two-burner stove, sink, propane heater, insulating blinds for the windows, hot water, bunk beds, and maybe even an actual toilet inside their home-on-wheels, of course.

boxing the needle

boxing the needle /ˈbäk-siṉ hə ˈnē-dᵊl/

verb: The process of aligning a compass's needle with magnetic north so you can determine where you took a wrong turn. If you're looking for a physical box, you'll probably end up even more lost; you should instead be putting the needle in the red drawn box called the orienting arrow. If you have no idea what a compass is or what it's doing in your hand, we've likely identified your first problem. If you didn't even bring a map, you're totally screwed.

brain /ˈbrān/ **noun:** The compartment sitting atop most larger backpacks that jiggles around like a bobblehead. A brain often includes one or two zippered pockets to stash important small items like car keys, trail maps, and GPS devices—basically, all the stuff that's critical for navigating, just like your own noggin. This brain's usually removable, though, so don't lose it.

break camp /ˈbrāk ˈkamp/ *verb:* To

dismantle and pack up all your campsite equipment, such as a tent, sleeping bag, camp table, and so on. Ideally, you're not breaking anything in the process, because camping gear is really expensive, and that's a surefire way to ruin an otherwise awesome weekend.

breathable /ˈbrē-thə-bəl/ *adjective:*

Describes a fabric's ability to allow moisture vapor to move through it. A breathable material will allow your body heat to escape instead of trapping it inside your rain jacket and turning said jacket into a sauna. In reality, however, breathability is a suspect claim. Raise your hand if you've ever climbed a mountain in a hard shell and thought to yourself, *Wow, wearing this jacket makes me feel like I'm in an air-conditioned room.* Yeah, me neither.

bug net /ˈbəg ˈnet/ *noun:* A complicated weave of fibers designed to prevent insects from making you a human smorgasbord.

bug spray /ˈbəg ˈsprā/ *noun:* A misty mix of various chemicals designed to hide your sweet eau de carbon dioxide and thus prevent insects from homing in on your precious flesh.

bugnado /bəg-ˈnā-(ˌ)dō/ *noun:* A swirling mass of flying insects that descend upon your campsite the moment you sit down to eat; known to cause erratic dancing, flailing, and sobbing.

Bureau of Land Management

/ˈbē ˈel ˈem/ *noun:* More commonly referred to as BLM; the government agency responsible for protecting millions of acres of public land and for ensuring that your favorite campsite is located 28 miles down a washboard road.

bushwhacking /ˈbu̇sh-ˌ(h)wa-kiŋ/ *verb:*

The art of heroically pretending you know where you're going while battling branches and cursing your own stubbornness.

C

cabin camping /ˈka-bən ˈkam-piŋ/ *verb:*

1. To camp, only with walls, a roof, a floor, a mattress, and maybe even electricity. Best for folks who prefer to snap photos of the stars through windows. **2.** The bold act of trading in tent stakes for bed pillows and calling it roughing it.

See also: glamping

cairn /ˈkern/ *noun:* A small stack of rocks marking the trail on hiking routes. These stone piles are meant to guide you to your destination but have a tendency to lead you directly toward nowhere.

camel up /ˈka-məl ˈəp/ *verb:* To engage in the ingenious thru-hiking practice of chugging gallons of water at every source just to avoid the sin of carrying an extra water bottle.

CamelBak /ˈka-məl-ˌbak/ *noun:*

Hydration royalty. A brand so iconic that you probably didn't even know you're using a pack manufactured by someone else; the Kleenex of hydration bladders.

See also: bladder

camp crust /ˈkamp ˈkrəst/ *noun:* **1.** A unique blend of sunscreen, dust, and dead bugs that collects on your skin throughout a camping trip. **2.** Nature's exfoliator.

camp gremlin /ˈkamp ˈgrem-lən/ *noun:* **1.** The mischievous creature responsible for hiding your camp spork, moving your headlamp, and (occasionally) misplacing one of your hiking socks. **2.** Your favorite camping friend who disappears when it's time to cook dinner but miraculously returns just as the soup is ready.

camp hero /ˈkamp ˈhir-(ˌ)ō/ ***noun:*** The saintly champion who does the Lord's work—e.g., makes breakfast in the predawn cold, pitches tents in the rain, or relocates creepy crawlies—while everyone else "supervises."

camp stove /ˈkamp ˈstōv/ ***noun:*** A portable, compact cooking device that runs on gas, liquid fuel, or sorcery. At-home dinners often require up to four burners to create culinary masterpieces, but camp stoves manage to conjur life-changing meals with just a single flame, a wind screen, and the faint smell of propane. Your grandma's kitchen has nothing on the gastronomic prowess of a creaky Coleman at suppertime.

camp stove fuel /ˈkamp ˈstōv ˈfyü(-ə)l/

noun: A prefilled and refillable bottle of fancy fuel. There's one designed for every camp stove and every occasion. Walk into any store and you'll see a million varieties of canisters and bottles in myriad colors on the shelves, just begging to burn your biscuits. Here are the differences between the two main types:

	Definition	**Fuel Composition**	**Pros**	**Cons**
Canister Fuel	Insta-fuel for the #vanlife crowd. Twist and go.	Packaged blend for your convenience: propane, butane, and isobutane.	Lightweight, easy, and idiot-proof. Great for lazy mornings and social media posts.	Costs more than a kid and hates the cold.
Liquid Gas	Requires dedication and commitment. It's a relationship.	Typically white gas— basically moonshine for your stove.	A cheap date if you're willing to commit. Reliable AF.	Requires a PhD to operate. Noisy enough to terrify the bears.

campervan /ˈkam-pər-ˌvan/ *noun:* A cramped shoebox on wheels, made newly popular by 21st-century adventurers seeking a minimalist approach to life by spending a small fortune on a vehicle that's twice the size of a normal car. Cheap and easy camping and/or parking spots include the brightly illuminated parking lots found at any Walmart or Cracker Barrel; there's nothing like corporate-subsidized minimalism to help you break free from the binding constraints of society, amiright?

campervan

campfire /ˈkamp-ˌfī(-ə)r/ *noun:* A controlled open-air fire in the middle of a campsite that will char marshmallows and leave your clothes reeking of smoke for at minimum a year. Unlike our ancestors, most modern campers do not use campfires for cooking or warmth; we have cars, campervans, and RVs for that, thank you very much. Instead, campfires have a certain je ne sais quoi. We don't even care if it's fire season—give us our damn ambience.

See also: car camping

campfire philosopher /ˈkamp-ˌfī(-ə)r fə-ˈlä-s(ə-)fər/ *noun:* A wilderness thinker who uses the crackle of the fire and the aroma of s'mores as the setting for their latest TED Talk.

camping /ˈkam-piŋ/ *verb:* A questionable activity in which people spend a lot of money, time, and effort to sleep outside in the dirt, wake up with a major crick in the neck, and wander around the woods whenever urination calls.

camping fee /ˈkam-piŋ ˈfē/ *noun:* **1.** A small payment that secures for you a tranquil patch of earth in a campground next to forty-seven RVs and three groups of partying fraternities. **2.** Evidence that even Mother Nature now has a cover charge.

campground /ˈkamp-ˌgraůnd/ ***noun:*** A designated plot of land where hundreds of people congregate to find solitude and quiet—away from other humans.

car camping /ˈkär ˈkam-piŋ/ ***verb:*** Sleeping outside in a location that is accessible by car. For some, it means sleeping *inside* your car. Either way, this approach usually involves cramming an ungodly amount of gear into your vehicle (a process known as "packing Tetris") so you can enjoy all your at-home luxuries while trying to reset from your daily life.

cathole /ˈkat-ˌhōl/ *noun:* A 6- to 8-inch hole that a camper digs in the ground to use as an outdoor restroom. A cathole is one of the best ways for your stomach's leftovers to decompose quickly and minimize the spread of disease. The challenge, however, is in hovering your hindquarters a few inches above the soil while playing target practice before sunrise.

See also: beaver fever, trowel

citronella /ˌsi-trə-ˈne-lə/ *noun:* A type of natural mosquito repellent sold in spray or candle form, often used by campers who prefer natural or nontoxic ingredients. You'll know you've found one of their camps when you spy multiple bags of granola, barefoot-style hiking sandals, and humans covered in angry red welts; recent science says citronella doesn't do much to deter those pterodactyl-sized bugs. You're just choosing to smell like grass.

C

cold soaking /ˈkōld ˈsō-kiŋ/ *noun:* **1.** A long, cold bath for dehydrated meals. **2.** A backpacker's solution for lightening a heavy pack that involves ditching the stove. The result: wallowing in the resplendent laziness of dining on frigid mush.

contour lines /ˈkän-ˌtu̇r ˈlīnz/ *noun:* The

tiny lines on a topographic map that connect points of equal elevation. By assessing these contours, hikers and campers can determine the shape and elevation of the terrain they're navigating and improve decision-making. Lots of lines packed closely together? That's a steep slope, and you'll probably fall off a cliff if you try to camp there. A series of concentric circles getting smaller and smaller? You're looking at the summit of a mountain, and if you put your tent there, pray that your deadman skills are better than your map-reading skills.

See also: deadman

compression sack /kəm-'pre-shən 'sak/

noun: A high-pressure hug for your sleeping bag. These drawstring sacks have side straps that miraculously squeeeeeeeeze the air from a sleeping bag until it shrinks from the size of a beach ball to Vin Diesel's biceps. This saves tons of space inside your backpack, but make sure you remove your sleeping bag after the camping trip. Smooshing it inside a compression sack for too long will damage the insulation. You've been warned—and Vin Diesel is watching.

cot /ˈkät/ **noun:** A raised camp bed that offers luxurious separation from the hard ground, along with a few extra pounds to carry and exactly zero insulation from the frigid air swirling beneath you.

cowboy camping / ˈkau̇-ˌbȯi ˈkam-piŋ/ **verb:** Sleeping outside without a shelter—by choice. Let's be clear: This does not make you a cowboy. You won't be riding any horses, and there is no sweet hat to give you trail cred. Instead, you're electing to snooze under the stars without a nylon fortress to protect you from the cruel realities of Mother Nature. Giddyup.

See also: bivouac

cowboy coffee /ˈkau̇-ˌbȯi ˈkȯ-fē/ *noun:*

A dubious concoction produced by dumping ground coffee into a pot of boiling water, then stirring the sludge before drinking it, hoping to avoid a mouthful of grinds. Serve it when you serenade your companions with old-timey campfire tunes because you've completely reverted back 200 years. Sure, cowboys did this a long time ago, but that was before the invention of the AeroPress or the Stanley PourOver. And for the love of all that's holy, have you never heard of instant coffee?

See also: instant coffee

cowboy coffee

cryptobiotic soil /ˈkrip-(ˌ)tō-bī-ˈä-tik ˈsȯi(-ə)l/ *noun:* The exact wrong place to pitch your tent. If you've ever heard anyone yelling "Don't step on the crypto!" and found yourself frantically eyeing the ground for loose digital currency, this definition is for you. Found in arid and semi-arid environments, cryptobiotic soil (crypto) is a blackened, sponge-like biological crust that includes countless tiny organisms and protects these fragile ecosystems. Just know that if you set up your tent in a patch of crypto, you'll have thousands of invisible, microbiotic aliens haunting you for the rest of your life because it takes decades or even centuries for the soil to recover.

Cuben Fiber /ˈkyü-bən ˈfī-bər/ *noun:*

1. A space-age fabric touted for its impressive durability, ultralight weight, and its innate ability to separate campers into two categories: those who "get it" and those who don't.
2. A subtle status symbol that lets other hikers know you blew your bank account before hitting the trail.

See also: ultralight

curfew /ˈkər-(ˌ)fyü/ *noun:* A friendly
suggestion from campground hosts indicating the start of quiet hours. Curfew typically commences with exactly zero people hushing up until the hosts show up with a flashlight and *that* look, making it clear that you are now the problem.

D

daypack /ˈdā-ˌpak/ *noun:* The
overachiever's fanny pack for day-long
adventures, filled with everything you need
except for that one thing. Packed properly,
the correct proportions are 30 percent extra
apparel, 30 percent snacks, 30 percent water,
and 10 percent existential dread from realizing
you don't actually know how to read a compass.

deadfall /ˈded-ˌfȯl/ *noun:* **1.** A chaotic mess of
downed trees and branches strewn across the
trail that you swore was marked "maintained."
2. Nature's way of suggesting you choose
another route.

See also: widow-maker

deadfall

deadman /ˈded-ˌman/ **noun: 1.** An anchor (a rock, log, filled stuff sack, etc.) used to secure one's tent to the ground when camping in snow, sand, or rocky environments where regular tent stakes will slip right out. To set up a deadman, bury it horizontally, rather like a coffin (this is all getting a little morbid and depressing). **2.** A pseudo–IQ test perfect for those moments when campers want to practice their knot-tying skills under pressure. After all, there is no greater penalty for failure than the realization that you had one job, screwed it up, and lost your tent to the gale-force winds.

dehydrated meal /(ˌ)dē-ˈhī-ˌdrā-təd ˈmēl/ *noun:*

A store-bought meal crammed inside pancake-flat packaging that's loaded with crunchy calories and obscene amounts of sodium but is completely devoid of any hydration (duh) or discernable flavor, regardless of what the description says. These are best enjoyed when your judgment is impaired and standards are lowered (i.e., in a delirious condition known as "backpacking").

dispersed camping /di-ˈspərst ˈkam-piŋ/ *verb:* **1.** To camp for free on public lands outside of a campground. This is the outdoors equivalent to a *Choose Your Own Adventure* gamebook, as you never know what you'll find at the end of the dirt road: It may be the most glorious campsite ever to grace the planet or a heavily wooded mountainous slope that requires you to tie your tent to a tree and conduct a 20-point turn to flip your car around. **2.** The ultimate exercise in optimism.

dome tent /ˈdōm ˈtent/ *noun:* A tent that looks like a dome. You're welcome.

double-wall tent /ˈdə-bəl-wȯl ˈtent/

noun: A type of camping shelter that has an internal layer with mesh walls and a second layer over the top, often a rain fly. These are ideal for group sleeping situations, since double walls and double doors make for quadruple the zippers. No one is sneaking out of this tent on your watch.

See also: rain fly, single-wall tent

draft collar /ˈdraft ˈkä-lər/ *noun:* An insulation-filled tube at the top of a sleeping bag that blocks chilly drafts, seals in warmth, and removes your sense of freedom.

duct tape

dry bag /ˈdrī ˈbag/ *noun:* A waterproof bag made from PVC, nylon, or coated vinyl that prevents your belongings from getting wet, even when camping in the middle of a thunderstorm. A dry bag is like a magical vault in which to throw your valuables, although you'll never be entirely sure when you'll find them again, no matter how much one-armed rummaging you can endure.

duct tape /ˈdək(t)- ˈtāp/ *noun:* An extra-sticky gray tape that can repair any problem on Earth, in space, and probably even beyond. When camping, duct tape is the universal fix-all—there is literally nothing it can't do, from patching a popped sleeping pad to stabilizing a backcountry splint if you get an owie. And, if you ask real nicely, duct tape may even take down your tent or carry you back to the trailhead.

dump station /ˈdəmp ˈstā-shən/ *noun:*

1. A necessary place of horrors where RVers can properly dispose of their wastewater.

2. A facility where #vanlife fantasies collide with reality as you manhandle tubes filled with your own doings and ponder what you ate to create that color.

See also: idiot check

Dutch oven /ˈdəch ˈə-vən/ *noun:* **1.** A cast-iron lidded pot with legs designed to sit above a campfire used for preparing camp meals that literally no one ever makes but look good on your favorite camp cooking website. **2.** The wretched but all-too-common scenario in which one camper breaks wind inside a double sleeping bag and then traps their companion inside with the deadly smell. This is especially horrific if the offending camper has been enjoying high-fiber foods or sodium-infused dehydrated meals for a few days.

DWR /ˌdē-ˌdə-bəl-(ˌ)yü-ˈär/ *noun:* An abbreviation for "durable water repellent," a magical chemical finish that turns your gear into a water-hating diva. If raindrops try to cling, DWR says, "Not today, Satan."

dyneema /dī-ˈnē-mə/ *noun:* An ultrafancy, ultradurable, and ultralight fabric beloved by ounce counters, gear snobs, and the type of campers who say "base weight" more than once in any given conversation.

E

elevation gain /ˌe-lə-ˈvā-shən ˈgān/ *noun:*

A number that tells you how high you'll climb and how much your legs will hate you by the end of your hike.

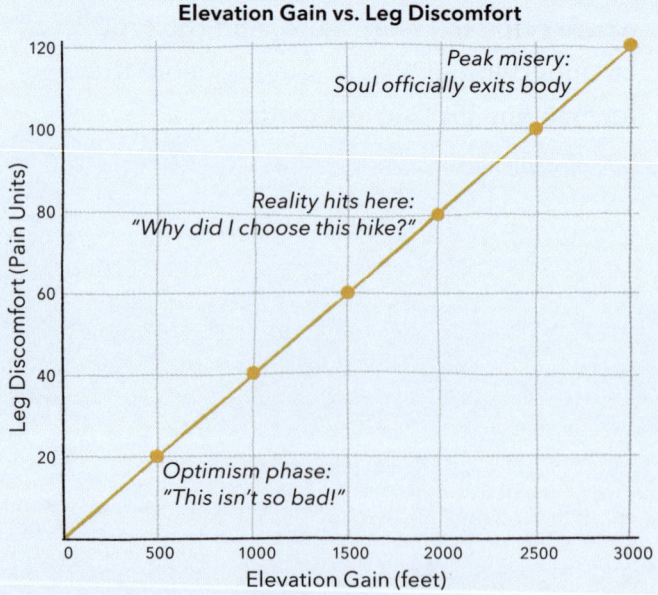

Elevation Gain vs. Leg Discomfort

Peak misery:
Soul officially exits body

Reality hits here:
"Why did I choose this hike?"

Optimism phase:
"This isn't so bad!"

Leg Discomfort (Pain Units)

Elevation Gain (feet)

embers /ˈem-bərz/ *noun:* Quiet, unassuming sparks of fire that provide joy and happiness until they locate your favorite camp chair and burn a hole in it.

See also: firestarter

established campsite

/i-ˈsta-blisht ˈkamp-ˌsīt/ *noun:* A patch of ground that has been officially designated by a mysterious "someone" as special dirt for anyone hoping to sleep on it.

See also: dispersed camping

F

facilitree /fə-ˈsi-lə-trē/ *noun:* 1. A tree that silently judges you while you turn its trunk into a personal lavatory. 2. A tree that has seen things—terrible, unspeakable, horrible things.

See also: tree pee

fall line /ˈfȯl ˈlīn/ *noun:* The natural downhill path that water (and maybe your body) wants to take. Skiers love it. Hikers fall down it.

facilitree

false summit /'fȯls 'sə-mət/ *noun:* The point when a hiker thinks they've reached the top of a mountain only to learn that they have farther to go. This soul-crushing realization is often accompanied by temper tantrums, feelings of regret, inconsolable frustration, and delightfully unique exclamations of profanity.

fanny pack /'fa-nē 'pak/ *noun:* A hip-hugging gear hauler that was once ridiculed but is now revered. Nothing screams "I don't care what you think" like a fanny pack.

fastpacking /ˈfas(t)-ˌpa-kiŋ/ *verb:* A hyper-speedy (and some say frantic) way to camp in mountain terrain, reminiscent of that '90s television show *Supermarket Sweep* where contestants maniacally ran around a grocery store gathering expensive items in an effort to tally up the highest bill—only without the supermarket and with a much higher price tag. Fastpacking combines backpacking with trail running; you still have to carry all your gear, but it won't weigh much because you'll likely cut your toothbrush in half to shave fractions of ounces from your load.

firestarter

firestarter /ˈfī(-ə)r-ˌstär-tər/ *noun:* **1.** A highly flammable substance used to light a campfire quickly so you don't spend your entire evening under the stars bemoaning your inability to burn wood. Unless you're MacGyver, you've probably never produced a flame with flint, and holding your lighter up against a twig for forty-two minutes until it finally catches isn't particularly effective, either. Instead, a handy firestarter will get the flames going to heat your weenies. **2.** The self-appointed leader of the flames.

See also: camp hero

F

fleece /ˈflēs/ *noun:* A miracle fabric that provides immense warmth, breathability, and durability so you can stay comfortable while sprinkling microplastics throughout the campsite.

See also: Leave No Trace

floor area /ˈflȯr ˈer-ē-ə/ *noun:* The amount of floor space in a tent. Just like realtors, tent brands and retailers hawk their products by touting square footage. (The average camper needs at least 14 square feet of floor space for tight living.) Good rule of thumb: Never trust the label. If the tent says it's built for three people, it's likely going to be more comfortable for two humans plus gear—unless you enjoy the feeling of being packed inside nylon like smoke-covered sardines.

foil dinner /ˈfȯi(-ə)l ˈdi-nər/ *noun:* A tasty meal enjoyed after a long day of hiking when you're so hungry that a charred packet of crinkly aluminum foil looks like a feast fit for royalty. The concept is simple: Throw a bunch of chopped vegetables and protein slices on some aluminum foil, then fold it into a mini-packet (kind of like the notes you used to pass in middle school) and place it on top of a grate on an open fire. Don't let hunger turn you into a ravenous beast with the telltale burned fingertips.

footbox /ˈfu̇t-ˌbäks/ *noun:* A cozy cocoon of warmth for your tootsies that feels much better than it sounds. Contrary to its harsh name, a footbox is the delightfully warm bottom section of your sleeping bag where your feet go to hibernate in their own private padded dungeon. It's snug, insulated, and just spacious enough to remind you that freedom is overrated when it's below freezing outside.

forage /ˈfȯr-ij/ *verb:* To artfully wander through the woods picking plants and mushrooms like a hyper-focused squirrel. Foraging is basically the camping version of grocery shopping, only with an ill-chosen berry poisoning you instead of high-fructose corn syrup.

See also: dehydrated meal

four-season tent /ˈfȯr-sē-zᵊn ˈtent/

noun: **1.** A year-round shelter designed to withstand gale-force winds and wintry blizzards. **2.** The desired shelter for campers who enjoy the mental gymnastics of believing that a millimeter of nylon is capable of separating you from Mother Nature's worst and is not just a glorified windbreaker.

See also: winter camping

freestanding tent /ˈfrē-ˈstan-diŋ ˈtent/

noun: The camping shelter show-off loudly proclaiming, "Look, Ma, no stakes!" right before a gusty wind blows it away.

See also: non-freestanding tent

freeze–dried meal /ˈfrēz-ˈdrīd ˈmēl/

noun: An ultralight, packable camping meal with 80 percent of its water weight removed. Freeze-dried meals offer scientific proof that flavor and hiking distance have an inverse relationship: The weird-smelling noodles with green specks and questionable meat lumps will taste far better after a long, rigorous hike than if you were to consume them after a short stroll.

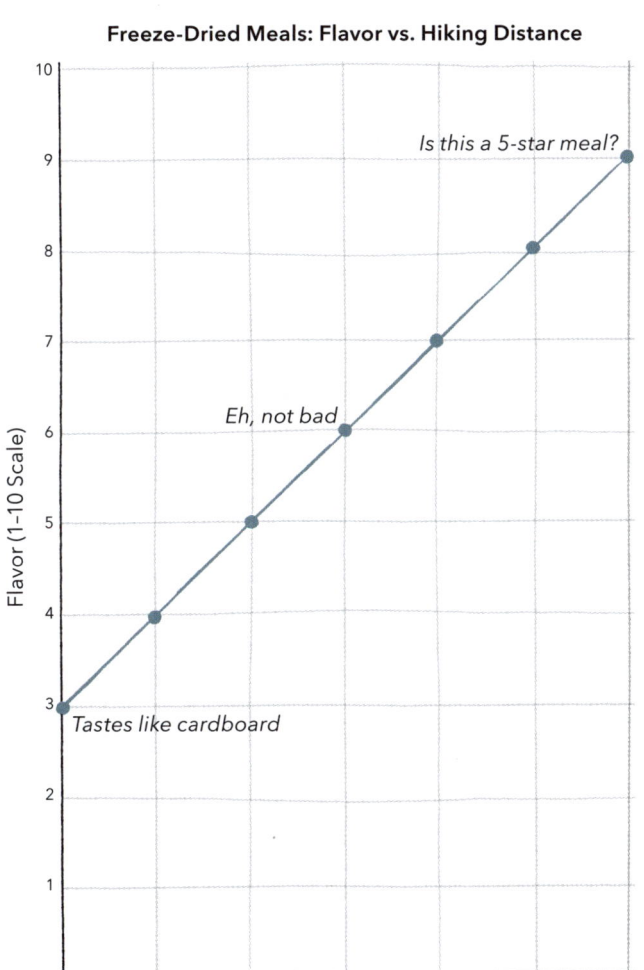

Freeze-Dried Meals: Flavor vs. Hiking Distance

Is this a 5-star meal?

Eh, not bad

Tastes like cardboard

Flavor (1–10 Scale)

Hiking Distance (miles)

frontcountry /ˈfrənt-ˌkən-trē/ *noun:* A
geographic region that offers car-accessible camping. Frontcountry campers are the well-adjusted geniuses who get to bring chocolate bars and bottles of wine to their campsite because their trusty steel steed is doing all the heavy lifting.

FU stop /ˈef-ˌyü ˈstäp/ *noun:* That time,
when hiking or backpacking, you struggle to keep up, fall behind, and then eventually reach your trail partner expecting a joyful reunion with rainbows and sunbeams pouring from the heavens—but instead, the cruel, inconsiderate scoundrel breaking trail immediately takes off again, barely giving you a moment to catch a single restful breath. It doesn't matter whether you call it a slinky stop, a Colorado stop, a safety meeting, the accordion effect, or the caterpillar effect—all an FU stop does is make you want to scream "f*ck you!!" at the top of your lungs.

frontcountry

full hookup /ˈfu̇l ˈhu̇k-ˌəp/ ***noun:*** **1.** A type of campsite geared toward RV campers that offers direct access to water, electricity, and a sewer. But if you're a tent camper who wants to spend a lot of money to stare at a few cables and tubes as part of your camping experience, go right ahead and snag a spot. The world is your utility oyster. **2.** A Tinder-arranged date with your bougiest sleep system.

See also: glamping

full-timer /ˈfu̇l-ˈtī-mər/ ***noun:*** A master of campground gossip and knowing the locations of the best free dump sites. These individuals live in their RVs year-round and can spot a free overnight site faster than you can put your car in park.

G

gear explosion /ˈgir ik-ˈsplō-zhən/

noun: The inevitable chaos that ensues upon returning from a camping trip when every piece of outdoor gear you own miraculously finds its way onto every surface in your home.

gear junkie /ˈgir ˈjəŋ-kē/ ***noun:*** **1.** A trail enthusiast who spends more time researching and collecting outdoor gear than actually camping. **2.** Anyone found inside an REI.

gear loft /ˈgir ˈlòft/ *noun:* A small scrap of mesh or nylon that hooks onto the ceiling of your tent, creating a tidy, tucked-away storage plateau that (marginally) capitalizes on unused space. It's yet another term yanked from the real estate industry that makes you think you're getting a lot when you're in fact getting quite little. Those expecting too much from a gear loft may ask, "Where is the entire second floor in my tent, accessed only by a ladder?"

gear shaming /ˈgir ˈshā-miŋ/ *verb:* A thinly veiled attempt to hide one's personal insecurities and validate the purchase of incredibly expensive gear by mocking or identifying defects in another's items.

What gear shamers are actually saying

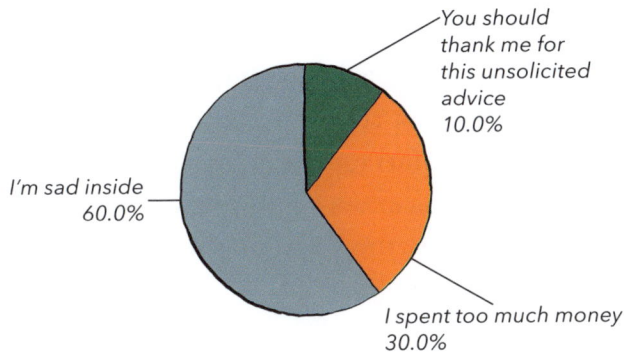

You should thank me for this unsolicited advice 10.0%

I'm sad inside 60.0%

I spent too much money 30.0%

giardia /jē-ˈär-dē-ə/ *noun:* **1.** A microscopic intestinal hitchhiker. **2.** Proof that no matter what that hardcore thru-hiker told you, water filters are not a waste of money.

glamping /ˈglam-piŋ/ *verb:* To camp in the outdoors with glamorous luxuries such as curated snacks, a cozy heating unit, Egyptian cotton sheets, hot running water, twinkly mood lights, and a safari tent large enough to fit two king-sized beds and a small seating area with tea service. But other than all that, it's exactly the same as camping.

gorp /ˈgȯrp/ *noun:* A popular trail-mix snack with an identity crisis. Although most hikers and campers pack gorp for their many adventures, experts aren't entirely sure what the acronym stands for. Some are firmly in the camp of "good ol' raisins and peanuts," while others are certain it's "granola, oats, raisins, and peanuts." But they're all wrong: Raisins are optional but M&M'S are mandatory.

GPS /jē-()pē-'es/ *noun:* An abbreviation for Global Positioning System. Campers and hikers use this satellite-based technology to navigate in the backcountry so they don't have to burden their busy 21st-century minds with the stress of learning how to read a topographic map or operate a compass. (It's a hardship, truly. So many squiggly lines and tiny ticks.)

GPS watch /jē-()pē-'es 'wäch/ *noun:* A wrist-worn device that tells you where you are in the world and tracks your pace, mileage, altitude, heart rate, step count, menstruation cycle, calories burned, weather trends, and even recovery time. There's nothing like an easy backpacking trip requiring twelve days of recovery to give you performance anxiety.

gram weenie /ˈgram ˈwē-nē/ *noun:*

A thru-hiker or backpacker who believes joy weighs too much. Possessions will include one shirt (with the tag cut off), one pot, and 17 spreadsheets back home detailing the weight of each item.

See also: ultralight

gravity water filter /ˈgra-və-tē ˈwȯ-tər ˈfil-tər/ *noun:* An idiot-proof filtration system that harnesses the superpowers of Earth's gravitational pull. Sure, it costs a little more than a standard manually operated water filter, but the ROI is huge when you factor in preventing all the emotional trauma that results from falling into a river every time you have to pump.

See also: water filter

group campsite /ˈgrüp ˈkamp-ˌsīt/ *noun:*

A campground where huge groups of friends can congregate. Typically identified by the large number of vehicles and small community of tents, group campsites are usually boisterous, chaotic, and packed with signs of civilization—perfect for a weekend respite in the natural world.

guyline /ˈgī-ˌlīn/ *noun:* A length of cord

attaching the outside of a tent to the ground. While guylines are useful for stabilizing structures in nasty weather, using them involves a test of knot-tying skills more challenging than the bar exam. And lest anyone think they can rest easy once they've managed the Herculean feat, don't forget about nightfall; once the sun goes down, guylines transform into a web of invisible ankle grabbers. (Pro tip: Regardless of how your bladder feels at midnight, you don't have to pee.)

H

hammock /ˈha-mək/ *noun:* 1. A fabric sling
stretched between two trees or other secure
points to create a cozy air couch. 2. A time-
sucking device that lures you in by promising
total comfort and relaxation while blissfully
gazing at the bluebird in the sky above in a
state of horizontal zen.

hand sanitizer /ˈhand ˈsa-nə-ˌtī-zər/ *noun:*
The alcohol-scented miracle gel that helps
you feel clean amidst seventy-two layers of
trail dirt.

See also: camp crust

hatchet /ˈha-chət/ *noun:* A tiny axe with big dreams, designed to demolish kindling and prove that size doesn't matter in the woods.

headlamp /ˈhed-ˌlamp/ *noun:* **1.** A hands-free light worn on one's head. **2.** The number one cause of temporary blindness among campers.

"hey, bear" /ˈhā ˈber/ *noun:* The traditional call used by campers spending time in grizzly bear territory. Despite what it sounds like, this call is *not* designed to welcome grizzlies to one's campsite. Instead, in a prime example of infallible human logic, it is thought to be an effective way to scare the 600-pound snuggle monsters and keep them from cozying up to you. Other popular calls include:

- "Dear God, that bear is huge!"
- "Get me out of here right now!"
- "This is the worst idea I've ever had!"
- Literally anything at full volume.

hiker hobble /ˈhī-kər ˈhä-bəl/ *noun:* **1.** The unmistakable waddle of someone who trudged 20 miles and now regrets everything. **2.** Post-trail swagger.

hiker hunger /ˈhī-kər ˈhəŋ-gər/ *noun:* That moment on a thru-hike when you realize a gas station hot dog and six Pop-Tarts were merely appetizers.

hiker midnight /ˈhī-kər ˈmid-ˌnīt/ *noun:* An informal phrase used to describe a camper's or hiker's bedtime after a long day on the trail. For the rest of the world, this witching hour is also called the "early bird special" or "dinnertime."

hiker trash /ˈhī-kər ˈtrash/ *noun:* **1.** A term of endearment describing those who spend months at a time living in the woods, forgoing showers, and groveling for food from total strangers. **2.** A human-shaped void fueled by Ramen noodles, packaged tuna, and gummy bears. **3.** Someone who soaks their food in cold water and calls it cuisine.

See also: cold soaking

hiking /ˈhī-kiŋ/ *verb:* The act of avoiding mainstream and urban pathways in favor of dirt ribbons that take the most circuitous, difficult routes to get you from point A to point B. Oftentimes, you end up where you started, wondering why your legs are so sore. Other times, you end up sunburned, covered in bug bites, more dehydrated than a raisin, and questioning that mysterious noise you heard half a mile back. No matter your final condition, when you think back, you'll smile, reminisce about the good times, and say, "Can't wait to do that again."

See also: Type II Fun

hip belt /ˈhip ˈbelt/ **_noun:_** A padded strap attached to the lower lumbar section of your pack that wraps around your hips and secures in the front of your body at your belly button, for better weight distribution, not unlike a straitjacket. Consider this an unflattering but well-meaning hug from your backpack.

hookup /ˈhu̇k-ˌəp/ **_noun:_** **1.** The magical touchpoint that brings water, electricity, and waste disposal to your RV so you don't have to pretend to rough it. **2.** The cute evening tête-à-tête happening over in Campsite 12.

See also: full hookup

idiot check /ˈi-dē-ət ˈchek/ *noun:* A final you've-done-it-already-but-need-to-do-it-again-because-what-if-you-forgot-your-favorite-tent-stake sweep of the campsite. Even if you think everything is packed into your vehicle or backpack and you're ready to leave camp, remember that gear has been known to grow its own legs and just . . . go somewhere else. Sleeping bags end up in trees. Headlamps hide under shrubs. Entire tents somehow waddle their way into the woods.

instant coffee /ˈin(t)-stənt ˈkȯ-fē/ *noun:*

The fast food of java. This nectar of the gods in the form of darkened sludge can be found at campsites 'round the world thanks to the simplicity of brewing with a teeny, tiny camp stove. It's easy: Boil your water, dump in the coffee grains, and voila! You've got yourself a hot cuppa caffeine, which may or may not be the only encouragement you need to disassemble that tent with numb fingers and nary a tantrum.

internal–frame backpack

/in-ˈtər-nᵊl ˈfrām ˈbak-ˌpak/ *noun:* **1.** A hiker's best friend, complete with a rigid interior structure designed to make you comfortable as you dump buckets of sweat while trekking uphill. **2.** The backpack that dethroned Grandpa's external rig.

J

jerky /ˈjər-kē/ *noun:* The official meat of the outdoors. Enough said.

jerry can /ˈjer-ē-ˌkan/ *noun:* A rigid water or fuel container often found at car campsites. If it's leaking or making a mess, it's usually yours.

Jetboil /ˈjet-bȯi(-ə)l/ *noun:* An integrated backpacking stove that combines the cooking pot and gas burner all into one tidy piece of equipment that, when operating, can somehow seem louder than a jumbo jet blasting down the runway.

K

kindling /ˈkin(d)-liŋ/ *noun:* The small twigs and other dry material used to start a campfire. While tiny and unassuming, this highly flammable pile of randomness gives every camper the opportunity to be a superhero. The first one to get a spark takes the cape.

KOA /ˈkā-ˈō-ˈā/ *noun:* The place to camp for people who don't like camping; stands for Kampgrounds of America. This national chain of privately owned, RV-oriented campgrounds stretches around the country in rugged and challenging landscapes like the parking lot of your favorite Kansas City diner or next to the ninth hole on the miniature golf course.

L

lantern /ˈlan-tərn/ *noun:* **1.** A lightbulb in a cage you can carry around camp so that you don't smash your foot into tent stakes in the dark. **2.** A huge attractant for every bug on Earth, so pick your poison: broken toes or mosquito bites. Your choice!

lean-to /ˈlēn-ˌtü/ *noun:* **1.** A three-sided structure with an overhanging roof that keeps your family from yelling at you when you forget the tent. They are typically found along trails in the northeastern United States, probably because they have too many trees and need to find a good use for them. **2.** Temporary makeshift structures, often with a tarp for a roof and open air on the sides. This is especially useful for when you forgot the tent *and* forgot to reserve the permanent lean-to. You're really crushing this camping thing, eh?

leapfrog /ˈlēp-ˌfrȯg/ *noun:* The unspoken contest between two strangers on a trail in an attempt to prove who is the stronger hiker. The battle often ends on the uphill stretch when both realize they are equally sad and suffering.

Leave No Trace (LNT) /'lēv 'nō 'trās/

noun: The most sacred and unimpeachable code of ethics for anyone who spends time in the outdoors. LNT has seven main principles designed to minimize human impact on nature:

1. Plan Ahead and Prepare
2. Travel and Camp on Durable Surfaces
3. Dispose of Waste Properly
4. Leave What You Find
5. Minimize Campfire Impacts
6. Respect Wildlife
7. Be Considerate of Other Visitors

(Translation: Don't be a tool; leave nature the same as you found it.)

long underwear /ˈlȯŋ ˈən-dər-ˌwer/ *noun:*

A mislabeled invention that is warm like pants
and named like underwear.

M

make camp /ˈmāk ˈkamp/ *verb:* The ironically phrased act of setting up your campsite. Assuming you're a civilized person following Leave No Trace principles, you're not actually "making" anything, since the second LNT guideline specifically states that in popular areas you should only camp in existing campsites. Still, you are making yourself a happy home for the night, so let's just say that counts.

marinate /ˈmer-ə-ˌnāt/ *verb:* To sit completely motionless in a camp chair while soaking in your own sweat and grime after a long hike. Typically accompanied by a thousand-yard stare and a snack you're too tired to chew.

merino /mə-ˈrē-(ˌ)nō/ **noun: 1.** Sheep wool so fancy that its innate properties (breathability, odor resistance, sustainability, unaffordability) have made it a miracle fiber touted by campers and hikers everywhere. **2.** A point of contention between those who merely like this fiber and those who won't stop talking about it.

See also: long underwear

mile /ˈmī(-ə)l/ **noun:** A measurement of trail torture with a fixed distance but a variable emotional toll; one mile may be the difference between having a good time and sending a letter home to your family that says, "Pitched my tent, not coming back. I live in the forest now."

multi-tool /ˈməl-tē-ˌtül/ **noun:** A pocket-sized gadget that promises to do everything yet generally remains folded up inside your backpack until you need it to stab at your bag of Ramen noodles.

mummy bag /ˈmə-mē ˈbag/ **noun:** A type of sleeping bag that tapers toward the foot and has a hood to pull over your head, resembling an ancient Egyptian mummy. *Not creepy at all.* While mummy bags are kryptonite for claustrophobic campers, their design serves a purpose: Less internal space keeps sleepers warmer than a rectangular bag while also providing the once-in-a-lifetime experience of snoozing inside a sarcophagus.

See also: rectangular bag

mummy bag

mushroom /ˈməsh-ˌrüm/ *noun:* The
mystery meat of the forest. A fungus can be
great for soups and salads or absolutely destroy
your camping weekend when you misidentify.
Forage carefully.

Mylar blanket /ˈmī-ˌlär ˈblaŋ-kət/ *noun:*
Also known as an emergency blanket or space
blanket; a shiny, crinkly, oversized piece of foil
that wraps you up and insulates you 'til you're
warmer than a baked potato.

N

Nalgene /ˈnal-jēn/ *noun:* A plastic used to make hugely popular reusable water bottles with a wide-mouth opening. Invented in 1949, Nalgene boomed in the late 1990s when campers and hikers realized they could literally spike the bottles off the summit of a mountain without breaking them. Today, they are best known for their innate ability to disappear just when you start packing, only to reappear six weeks later with a mysterious green fuzz growing on the inside.

national parks /ˈna-sh(ə-)nəl ˈpärks/ *noun:*

Dubbed "America's Best Idea," these federally protected areas were designed to preserve our natural wilderness and make outdoor recreation available to everyone—including the endlessly snaking conga line of people along the trails.

See also: public land

nero day /ˈnē-(ˌ)rō ˈdā/ *noun:* A day of thru-hiking identified by what it isn't: neither a rest day nor a full day of marching. It's a nearly zero day that's grappling with its identity like an awkward middle child.

See also: zero day

no-see-um /nō-ˈsē-əm/ *noun:* A tiny, barely visible biting bug often found in coastal areas. Proving that size really doesn't matter, these stealthy insects leave behind clusters of fiery welts that you won't see coming until they're covering your skin. You're probably itchy just reading this.

non-freestanding tent

/ˈnän-ˌfrē-stan-diŋ ˈtent/ *noun:* A type of small, lightweight, and exceedingly complicated tent requiring staked-out guylines or trekking poles to achieve enough tension to remain upright. Non-freestanding tents are also super fun to pitch in a rainstorm—it's just you against the nylon while Mother Nature dumps on you. Sure, you gain a lighter pack by eschewing tent poles, but you lose your dignity the first time an entire campground watches you fumble around trying to pitch that sucker.

See also: freestanding tent

no-see-um

norovirus /ˈnȯr-ə-ˌvī-rəs/ *noun:* The gastrointestinal saboteur of thru-hiker campgrounds. This overcompensating stomach bug can't decide if it wants to leave you curled up in your sleeping bag or sprinting to the outhouse—so it does both, on repeat.

See also: giardia

Nuptse /ˈnəp-sē/ *noun:* **1.** A mountain in the Khumbu region of the Himalayas. **2.** A type of puffer jacket commonly found on trails, in coffee shops, and wrapped around people who say things like "Yeah, I totally camp."

O

offseason /ˈȯf-ˌsē-zᵊn/ *noun:* The dead zone of camping. In much of the country, the offseason occurs during the winter months, when most humans really, really don't even want to go *near* a campground, and sleeping outside is akin to turning into a popsicle. In other parts, the offseason features scorching summer temperatures that will melt a tent's nylon onto your sweat-covered face. One benefit of camping when even the animals are snubbing the Great Outdoors is you'll save some hard-earned cash—unwanted things are cheap.

See also: peak season

P

peak bagger /ˈpēk ˈba-gər/ *noun:* 1. A dedicated hiker who enjoys standing atop mountains more than actually hiking them. 2. A data-obsessed outdoorist with an affinity for spreadsheet validation.

peak season /'pēk 'sē-zᵊn/ *noun:* **1.** When every camper with a tent and a dream decides it's *their* weekend to find serenity and solitude alongside five hundred of their closest friends. **2.** The campsite Hunger Games.

See also: offseason

pee cloth /'pē 'klȯth/ *noun:* Reusable toilet paper for anyone who needs to squat while they pee. The best pee cloths have fun or unique designs that spark joy, even while you're accidentally peeing on yourself in a windstorm. In a pinch, it can also double as a hot mitt, sweat rag, or even a koozie. Hopefully this goes without saying, but a pee cloth should probably be clean if you're going to use it to mop your forehead, but that's entirely your life choice.

pee funnel /ˈpē ˈfə-nᵊl/ *noun:* A funnel-shaped tool that allows all people to pee while standing; also known as a female urination device. This is especially useful when camping near poison ivy or when it's pouring rain and there is a zero percent chance you're going outside your tent. Peeing in a bottle just got a lot easier.

permit /ˈpər-mit/ *noun:* A document that allows you to camp legally in a designated area. Often plated in gold and kept safer than some state secrets, camping permits are highly sought after for popular national parks and wilderness areas. After all, nothing says finding solitude in the wilderness like navigating the red tape of government bureaucracy.

permit

pit toilet /ˈpit ˈtȯi-lət/ *noun:* A literal hole in the ground with a structure built over it. Pit toilets are commonly found at campgrounds and are easily identifiable thanks to the campers who kick the door open as they retreat from the premises, often with one hand covering their noses and a look of abject horror upon their faces. There is no running water or toilet paper, and experts recommend that you do not—under any circumstances—look down into the pit.

See also: Type III Fun

pocketknife /ˈpä-kət-ˌnīf/ *noun:* Not just a knife but also a can opener, marshmallow stick, whittling tool, temporary tent stake, chef's utensil, wine opener, screw tightener, and kindling chopper; a tiny blade with a massive ego.

point-to-point /ˈpȯint-tə-ˈpȯint/ *noun:* A type of hike that begins at one location and ends at another, presenting one of the unsolved mysteries of the camping world: What do you do when you reach the end? Do you turn around and return to camp or go wandering aimlessly through the wilderness? Keep walking until you reach the next town? Sit on a log and cry from the sheer emotional distress of indecision? No one knows.

pole clip /ˈpōl ˈklip/ *noun:* A small C-shaped device that secures tent poles to the body of the tent, helping to create the structure. While recent technological innovation has made pole clips ultralight and incredibly strong, experts still don't know how to avoid the blinding fingertip pain from removing pole clips in cold weather. Origami-like dexterity is required; use at your own discretion.

pole sleeve /ˈpōl ˈslēv/ **_noun:_ 1.** A small tunnel of fabric sewn into the tent through which the poles pass. Pole sleeves create a sturdier tent than clips because they distribute tension more evenly. **2.** A tent feature that turns your tent-pitching experience into a frustrating labyrinth of self-doubt.

postholing /ˈpōst-ˌhō-liŋ/ **_verb:_** To make the excellent decision to go on a hike, tromp through some late-season snow, and fall through the crunchy surface to reveal a depth akin to the seventh circle of hell. A hiker may sink to their ankles or descend to their hip bones; no one can predict except the almighty Mother Nature.

potable water /ˈpō-tə-bəl ˈwȯ-tər/ *noun:*

Drinkable water at campgrounds. (Say it with us: poh-tuh-buhl. Now say it again. And one more time for good measure. DID YOU SAY IT?!) Potable water is the good stuff—not laced with viruses, disease, and who knows what else. You'll also see non-potable water at campgrounds, meant to be used in RVs or trailers for gray or black water tanks. As obvious as it may seem, please only drink the potable water. Otherwise, your camping trip won't be the only thing painfully ripped to shreds.

See also: black water

public land /ˈpə-blik ˈland/ *noun:* The

crown jewel of camping (and thus, this book).
Most American camping takes place on public
lands such as state parks, national parks,
United States Forest Service (USFS) land,
or Bureau of Land Management (BLM)
land—all a massive playground that's open
to anyone who wants to use it. It's important
to understand the difference between public
land and private land, especially if you like
dispersed camping. Pitching your tent on
BLM public land, for instance, will garner
you epic sunrises and a dazzling night sky,
whereas camping on private land may land
you in handcuffs.

See also: dispersed camping

puffer /ˈpə-fər/ *noun:* An insulated jacket meant to keep you warm while playing outside. Puffers are stuffed with down or synthetic insulation, and packability and warmth vary depending on the type you purchase and level of bougie you aim to achieve. Be sure to put on your jacket whenever struggling to light a campfire—glowing-hot embers are drawn to these highly flammable garments, so that's sure to get the fire roaring.

Q

quiet hours /ˈkwī-ət ˈau̇(-ə)rz/ *noun:*

Enforced nap time at the campground. The hours of 10 p.m. to 8 a.m. are typically when we're all asked to tone down the noise, though toddlers of course neither read the signs nor believe in following the rules. The same may be said of the guy with the loud boombox camping next to you, but that's the price of admission when you seek solitude in a plot of nature with an urban density greater than Chicago.

quilt /ˈkwilt/ *noun:* The lovechild of a sleeping

bag and a blanket. Lighter than a sleeping bag and warmer than a blanket, a quilt features an open bottom, so you can live dangerously by kicking a leg out at night.

See also: R-value

R

R-value /'är-ˌval-(ˌ)yü/ *noun:* A term that
indicates thermal resistance but really boils
down to "how well do you want to sleep
tonight?" Sleeping pads with higher numbers
will keep you warmer while lower values may
indicate that the pad is nothing more than
a slight decorative barrier between you and
hypothermia.

rain fly /'rān 'flī/ *noun:* A rain jacket for your
tent. Unless you set it up wrong, in which case
it's more of a splash guard.

rectangular bag /rek-ˈtaŋ-gyə-lər ˈbag/

noun: A type of sleeping bag shaped like a rectangle. (Is your mind blown?) Unlike mummy bags, rectangular bags allow campers more wiggle room for nighttime acrobatics thanks to the wider footbox.

See also: mummy bag, footbox

reservation fee /ˌre-zər-ˈvā-shən ˈfē/

noun: A payment, often referred to as an outdoor tax, that is required to reserve a campsite in advance. What you actually reserve: a small patch of ground for your tent, maybe a picnic table and fire ring, and a lone parking spot for your vehicle. If you want to see wildlife or commune with nature, that will cost extra.

S

SAR /'es-ā-är/ *noun:* The commonly used acronym for Search and Rescue operations, also known as the "you screwed up and we're coming to save you" team. They are 100 percent judging all of us for our terrible life choices and lack of discernible skills when we get lost, injured, or otherwise imperiled, but at least they'll bail us out while doing it.

shoulder season /'shōl-dər 'sē-zⁿn/

noun: The period of time sandwiched smack in between peak season and offpeak season. In mountain environments, this is often considered to be spring or fall. One may think it's the worst time to go out into the woods—it's far from party time, after all—but shoulder season is like the secret handshake of camping: Once you know about it, you're in the club. (Calling it "mud season" will score you bonus street cred with the mountain town locals.) Sure, you may need some extra layers or a stronger constitution, but you'll be rewarded with fewer people and quieter campgrounds. And, yeah, maybe some mud.

See also: offseason, peak season

sidewall /ˈsīd-ˌwȯl/ *noun:* The vertical
swaths of fabric that form the walls of the tent. Sidewalls are the last line of defense against sideways rain, gusty winds, rogue insects, and creeper eyeballs that may be straying from the campsite next door.

single–wall tent /ˈsiŋ-gəl-wȯl ˈtent/ *noun:*
A type of camping shelter consisting of only a single layer, proving that humankind often struggles to do hard things. Single-wall tents are often lighter than double-wall tents—less stuff weighs less—but you'll likely pay the price with the sheer volume of sweat that pours from your body as you realize how muggy and hot you are inside.

See also: double-wall tent

slackpacking /ˈslak-ˌpa-kiŋ/ ***verb:*** The art of handing over your camping gear to a host who moves it from campsite to campsite; the glamping version of thru-hiking. Somewhere along the way, some geniuses realized that the fun parts of thru-hiking were trekking along the trails and camping under the stars—not breaking your spinal column by carrying all your worldly possessions in a monstrous pack. So, they took out the gross part and created slackpacking. In extra bougie circumstances (maybe involving cold, hard cash or just an insane amount of kindness), the hosts will even set up your camp!

See also: glamping

sleep clothes /ˈslēp ˈklōz/ *noun:* A sacred set of garments reserved for bedtime only. Never worn while hiking, eating, sweating, or even thinking about trail dust. Think of them as your tent tuxedo.

sleep system /ˈslēp ˈsi-stəm/ *noun:* An overcomplicated nap kit. Three things are needed for a cozy night of sleep outside: a sleeping pad, a sleeping bag, and a camp pillow. This trio of goods is considered a "system" only because some campers have an insatiable knack for fiddling with small details.

sleeping bag /ˈslē-piŋ ˈbag/ *noun:* A

portable, insulated cocoon designed to keep
you warm at night and packaged up like a
bear-sized hot dog.

sleeping bag liner /ˈslē-piŋ ˈbag ˈlī-nər/

noun: A thin sleeping bag for your sleeping bag; the Russian nesting dolls of camping. Not only do these lightweight cloth sacks add anywhere from 5 to 15 degrees of warmth to your snooze, they also prevent your body's dirt and oils from greasing up and ruining your sleeping bag. Bonus: You can use a liner all by itself when camping in warm conditions or to protect yourself from any suspicious crawling going on in hostel or motel beds.

sleeping pad /ˈslē-piŋ ˈpad/ **noun:** A mat

with delusions of grandeur and just enough padding and warmth to convince campers that sleeping on rocks *is* a good idea.

See also: R-value

s'more /'smȯr/ *noun:* **1.** A campfire culinary masterpiece that will always have campers asking for "some more" until they puke. **2.** A character indicator based on 'mallow preferences. Those with adventurous and impulsive spirits may prefer charred and flaming marshmallows, while campers with attention to detail and infinite patience opt for lightly browned.

s'morgasm /ˈsmȯr-ˌga-zəm/ *noun:* A fleeting sugar high that is tantamount to a culinary climax.

snackcident /ˈsnak-sə-dənt/ *noun:* **1.** A seemingly harmless snack break that escalates quickly into the frenzied consumption of every calorie in your backpack. **2.** A hiker's greatest shame.

spork /ˈspȯrk/ *noun:* A gadget you never knew you needed. Is it a spoon? Is it a fork? It's both—a spoon with small tines. Or maybe it's neither, since the fork function is questionable at best. But, hey, it's camping—you can always just dig your face into your dinner like a pig at a trough, and no one will dare question you.

spork

stargaze /ˈstär-ˌgāz/ *verb:* The romanticized act of lying on the ground and staring at the night sky while ignoring everything else happening at the campsite, including the insects scurrying onto your legs. If you engage in this nighttime meditation for too long, it may not dawn on you until the next morning that you willingly chose to sleep outside with the bears.

stuff sack /ˈstəf ˈsak/ *noun:* A small drawstring bag designed by the benevolent camping gods to hold bulky items like sleeping bags. Cramming a sleeping bag into a backpack without a stuff sack is like forcing a toddler into a snowsuit: awkward and cumbersome.

See also: compression sack

sufferfest /ˈsə-fər-ˌfest/ *noun:* **1.** A voluntary period of prolonged suffering in the outdoors that may include sleeping on uneven ground, enduring a barrage of bug bites, waking to freezing temperatures, pushing your muscles to their limit, abandoning personal hygiene, pooping in the woods (and then carrying that poop *out* of the woods), and completely disconnecting from all forms of civilization. **2.** Camping.

See also: Type II Fun

summit fever /ˈsə-mət ˈfē-vər/ *noun:* **1.** When logic takes a backseat to the need for a selfie at the top of a mountain. **2.** The hiking equivalent of "just one more episode."

See also: peak bagger

swamp crotch /ˈswämp ˈkräch/

noun: When your underwear reaches that unfortunate saturation point where it becomes a full-blown ecosystem. Can be treated with Gold Bond, river dips, or walking like you just rode a horse to camp.

switchback /ˈswich-ˌbak/ ***noun:*** Hiking's cruelest optical illusion—you keep hiking, yet the summit never gets any closer.

synthetic insulation

/sin-ˈthe-tik ˌin(t)-sə-ˈlā-shən/ ***noun:*** Human-made insulation used in sleeping bags and jackets. Unlike your morale, it doesn't mind getting wet.

T

tarp /ˈtärp/ *noun:* A waterproof square of fabric commonly used as a minimalist shelter by campers who think a whole tent is too darn luxurious and instead opt for nothing more than a small roof to cover their head and body. A tarp is the chameleon of outdoor shelters because you can pitch it with trekking poles, sticks, or tentpoles, or even string it up between a few trees if you're trying to impress Bear Grylls.

technical /ˈtek-ni-kəl/ *adjective:* A descriptor used to justify a $500 jacket that comes with its own instruction manual.

temperature rating /ˈtem-pər-ˌchu̇r ˈrā-tiŋ/ *noun:* **1.** A bold numerical ranking system devised by sleeping bag manufacturers that purports to provide the temperature at which you may or may not turn into a popsicle in one of their products. **2.** The gear equivalent of "Trust me, you'll be fine."

ten essentials /ˈten i-ˈsen(t)-shəlz/ *noun:* Your supposed insurance policy for outdoor playtime. Somewhere out there, a group of fancy outdoor experts got together and decided that equipment within these ten gear categories are the must-have basics to keep you safe during any camping adventure.

In no particular order, here are the Ten Essentials for your Get Outdoors Starter Pack:

Navigation
Really, you haven't learned to use a map and a compass yet?

Fire
Narrowly surpasses the wheel for humanity's greatest discovery.

Illumination
Sure beats wandering around in the dark.

Shelter
Better than a carefully placed batch of twigs that you'll Survivor into a crafty lean-to.

Sun Protection
The '80s called and want their tanning beds back.

Nutrition
"We don't even make it to the stop sign without a snack."

Repair Kit
How about a nice game of "how many items can we break on our first camping trip"?

Hydration
Shriveling up like a raisin because you ran out of water isn't particularly fun.

First Aid
An ouch-pouch when you trip over your tent's guylines and pitch headfirst into the picnic table.

Human Wrapping Paper
Every camper lives in a place with the worst weather in the country—just ask them!—so plan ahead.

tent envy

tent /'tent/ *noun:* A portable fabric shelter that allows campers to sleep within wispy-thin walls where large animals such as bears and wolves will never, ever find them.

tent envy /'tent 'en-vē/ *noun:* That demoralizing feeling you get when you realize your camping buddy's freestanding tent looks like a nylon palace with ample headroom, an oversized vestibule, and kingly double doors, while yours resembles a trash bag propped up with sticks.

See also: vestibule

tent footprint /ˈtent ˈfu̇t-ˌprint/ *noun:*

1. A protective covering that sits between your tent and the ground that's designed to prevent sharp objects from ripping your shelter to shreds.

2. What separates the gear purists from the heathens who pitch their tents on pine cones with nary a concern. You'll know if you're in the presence of a footprint user by their sparkly clean camp stove, impeccably rolled sleeping pads, and carefully swept campsite.

See also: gear junkie

thru–hike /ˈthrü ˈhīk/ *noun:* An end-to-end backpacking trip that never ends. If it somehow does conclude, however, you will have covered two million miles, lost all of your toenails, and completely drained your bank account (but at least you'll have some wicked calf muscles).

tinder /ˈtin-dər/ *noun:* The campfire's hype man who shows up to get the party started, burns brightly for a few blinding minutes, and then ghosts everyone by leaving the rest of the work to the kindling.

toy hauler /ˈtȯi ˈhȯ-lər/ *noun:* A trailer or specialized RV that makes transporting motorized toys possible—basically, a towable garage for motorheads who under no circumstances will go camping without a half-dozen different engines. Typically, toy haulers feature a drop-down wall so you can drive your gadget—snowmobile, ATV, motorcycle, dirt bike, Smart car, pogo stick, whatever—onto the platform. What you won't find in the toy hauler: anything without a motor. Clearly, camping isn't camping without an engine that goes "ROAR."

trail angel /ˈtrāl ˈān-jəl/ *noun:* The fairy godmothers of hiking, only they come packing snacks instead of wands.

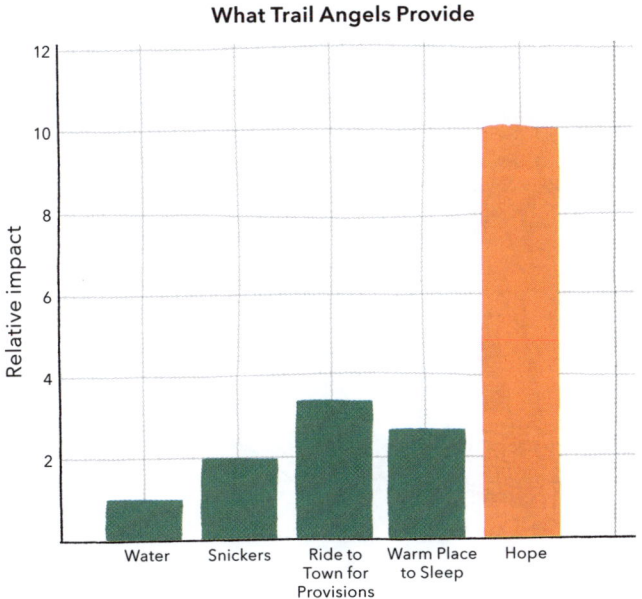

What Trail Angels Provide

trail family

trail family /ˈtrāl ˈfam-lē/ *noun:* A ragtag crew of hikers who start as complete strangers but end the journey as each other's personal therapists and cheering squad. You don't quite choose them, but you can't live without them. They're the only ones who know why you smell as bad as you do.

trail legs /ˈtrāl ˈlegz/ *noun:* **1.** A condition that marks a miraculous rite of passage in which a hiker's legs graduate from saying, "What is wrong with you?" to "Bring it on, mountain." **2.** The wobbly, newborn deer style of walking through town that indicates you have no recollection of how flat ground works.

See also: thru-hike

trailhead /ˈtrāl-ˌhed/ *noun:* The charming spot where you wave goodbye to all forms of civilization and say hello to sleepless nights, mosquito infestations, and the occasional ursine companion sniffing around your backpack.

tree pee /ˈtrē ˈpē/ *noun:* **1.** A nature lover's bathroom break. **2.** A camper's version of marking their territory.

See also: facilitree

trowel /ˈtrau̇(-ə)l/ *noun:* A small hand shovel ideal for camping. One must dig a 6- to 8-inch hole to use as a poop receptacle so one's feces decomposes before the neighborhood bear gets curious about yesterday's lunch. Pro tip: If there is poop on the trowel, you're doing it wrong.

See also: cathole

Type I Fun /ˈtīp ˈwən ˈfən/ ***noun:*** Activities or experiences that are enjoyable while you're doing them. Examples include:

- Pooping in the woods (you're never freer)
- Watching your friend invent new curse words while pitching the tent as you relax on a picnic table with a can of sparkling water and a delectable snack
- Riding your bike around the campground loop at top speed while yelling, "We all paid for this, suckers!"

Type II Fun /ˈtīp ˈtü ˈfən/ *noun:* Activities or experiences that are enjoyable in retrospect but had definite moments of suckiness while doing them. Examples include:

- Collapsing in relief at the top of Mount Katahdin after thru-hiking the Appalachian Trail, and realizing you no longer have to do the thing anymore because they spent every night of the last six months pitching a tent, often in the pouring rain, and witnessing spectacles like gale-force winds carrying away their favorite rain jacket

- Literally any activity listed in this book

Type III Fun /ˈtīp ˈthrē ˈfən/ *noun:* Activities or experiences that are enjoyable neither in the moment nor in retrospect. There is no pleasure to be found in Type III Fun, and it's unclear why the word "fun" is even used in this context. Examples include:

- Enduring a bivouac in the middle of a lightning storm on the side of a mountain

- Sailing to Antarctica with Ernest Shackleton and getting your boat stuck in the ice before seeking refuge on a deserted island

- Accidentally camping on a hill of red ants and not realizing it until you've delicately slipped inside your sleeping bag and your skin starts to feel blowtorched

See also: cowboy camping

U

ultralight /ˈəl-trə-ˌlīt/ *adjective:* Describes a style of backpacking that involves carrying the absolute lightest, most featherweight gear possible. Unlike standard lightweight backpacking, ultralight proponents are willing to ditch durability, comfort, and a decent amount of self-respect in favor of toting the teeny-tiniest pack on the trail. You'll know you've encountered one of these ounce counters by the look of longing on their face when you roll into camp, chomping on a chocolate bar, swigging whiskey from a flask, and unfurling your full-length, heavy-duty sleeping pad from the 1960s.

See also: gram weenie

ultralight

V

variable conditions /ˈver-ē-ə-bəl kən-ˈdi-shənz/ *noun:* A catchall phrase used by meteorologists and optimistic trip leaders that roughly translates to "no one has a clue what the weather is going to do, so prepare to suffer."

vault toilet /ˈvȯlt ˈtȯi-lət/ *noun:* The still horrific but more permanent solution to the campground toilet quandary. A vault toilet is one step above a pit toilet since it isn't *just* a hole in the ground: It includes a container that holds all the partially digested hot dogs that your intestines struggled with the night before. For wholesome family campground entertainment, consider inviting your kids to watch the maintenance team empty it with their high-powered machinery.

See also: pit toilet

"very close" /ˈver-ē ˈklōz/ *adjective:* Trail speak for "I don't actually know how much farther it is, but I want you to keep going!"

vestibule /ˈve-stə-ˌbyül/ *noun:* The mudroom for your tent home. Usually constructed using the rainfly, a vestibule is a covered area just outside the door to your tent that is used to stash wet gear, mucky boots, and any dirty object that you're hoping to keep out of the inner nylon sanctum. (Unfortunately, your kids get to come inside.)

See also: tent envy

W

WAG bag /'wag 'bag/ *noun:* A receptacle that backcountry campers use to carry their poop out of sensitive wilderness areas, not unlike the little plastic bags that dog owners use after Fido lets it fly on the neighbor's lawn. WAG stands for Waste Alleviation and Gelling; the magical powder inside the bag begins to neutralize, solidify, and decompose your body's leftovers. If it makes your butt wiggle like your favorite furry friend, that's just an added bonus.

walk–in site /'wȯk-ˌin 'sīt/ *noun:* A campsite not accessible by vehicle, which means you'll be carrying your gear a "short distance" that feels more like a portage across a hostile planet.

walking stick /ˈwȯ-kiŋ ˈstik/ *noun:* An implement used to provide balance and support on the trail so you can pretend like you're not out of breath every five seconds.

wash station /ˈwȯsh ˈstā-shən/ *noun:* **1.** A shared campground sink meant for brushing teeth and other forms of personal hygiene. **2.** A shared campground sink *not* meant for aggressively scrubbing your marinara-stained pot while pretending to have missed the "no dishwashing" sign.

See also: potable water

water filter /ˈwȯ-tər ˈfil-tər/ **_noun:_** A handy device that acts as a bouncer for your GI tract by kicking out every germ, virus, and questionable speck of grossness that has entered your drinking water. Whether you're camping in the backcountry without access to fresh water or your campground's spigot is growing a suspicious green mold, a water filter ensures that your biggest camping drama is that sweet hiker's tan—and not a parasite-induced midnight wakeup call.

See also: beaver fever

water resistant /ˈwȯ-tər ri-ˈzi-stənt/ **_adjective:_** A term describing a type of gear that sometimes makes you happy by shedding moisture, but other times leaves you soaked, sad, abandoned, and lonely; it's the great unknown of your camping kit—until it rains.

water filter

waterproof/breathable

/ˈwȯ-tər-ˌprüf ˈbrē-t͟hə-bəl/ ***adjective:*** **1.** A term describing a type of gear that theoretically will manage to keep you completely dry and, at the same time, allow water vapor to escape through the fabric, preventing moisture buildup. **2.** One of the greatest lies in all the camping kingdom.

web walker /ˈweb ˈwȯ-kər/ ***noun:*** The trail-breaking superhero of any backpacking trip who takes one for the team by plowing their face into all the spider webs. Depending on where you live and how far into the unholy wilderness you've decided to go, there is a strong chance that your trekking route will be littered with all forms of wildlife—especially in the morning when the world is just waking up. Top of the list: spiders. This means the person at the front of your group must accept the inevitable: a stringy-and-wet spiderweb stretched across their eyeballs. What a way to wake up.

weekend warrior /ˈwēk-ˌend ˈwȯr-ē-ər/
noun: You. Me. Probably anyone reading
this book, because for most of the working
world, we get only the weekends: that blessed
Saturday-Sunday combination when we can
finally hit the trail, sleep outside, and post all
the best snaps online so our coworkers see how
cool we are when we're away from our desks.
If that sounds like you, continue conquering
the weekend, you little Viking.

wet wipe /ˈwet ˈwīp/ *noun:* **1.** A small, pre-
moistened tissue that claims to wipe away
the trail grime but mostly just smears the dirt
around like a crappy wilderness shower. **2.** A
portable guilt trip that silently judges your
every swipe as you add to an overflowing
landfill in the name of clean armpits.

WFA /ˈdə-bəl-(ˌ)yü ˈef ˈā/ *noun:* Stands for Wilderness First Aid, a 16-hour training course for casual campers to learn how to deal with basic outdoor emergencies. Because nothing says "relaxing hobby" like splinting your friend's leg with a trekking pole.

WFR /ˈdə-bəl-(ˌ)yü ˈef ˈär/ *noun:* An acronym for Wilderness First Responder, an 80-hour intensive training course designed to prepare serious campers for medical emergencies in remote regions; pronounced "woofer" but is not a dog. You'll never need to ask which person in your posse carries this prestigious certification because they'll be sure to tell you upon first meeting.

WFR and WFA are often confused, so here is a chart to explain the differences:

	WFA	**WFR**
Duration of Course	A weekend to remember	More than a week of busted friends and fake blood
Who It's For	Campers who want to stay less than an hour from civilization	Campers who want to free their minds, ditch humanity, and disappear off grid
Medical Equipment	Band-Aids for boo-boos	Field surgery with your tweezers, a tarp, and a dirty shoelace
End Results	"I can splint your sprain with my spork!"	"I can reset your busted femur before carrying you out of the Grand Canyon on my back!"

widow-maker

widow–maker /ˈwi-dō-ˌmā-kər/ *noun:*

1. A sketchy tree or branch that is still standing but shouldn't be. You'll sometimes hear these suckers creaking in the wind as they pit their last dregs of resistance against the earthly pull of gravity. It's never a good idea to hike near a widow-maker, but the real concern is camping beneath one: Just don't. **2.** Not a heart attack, although it could give you one.

See also: deadfall

winter camping /ˈwin-tər ˈkam-piŋ/

noun: **1.** When you swap sleeping in the dirt for sleeping in the snow, armed with overpriced gear and a puzzling sense of adventure. **2.** An exercise in backpedaling once you realize your sleeping bag will never be warm enough.

Y

yogi–ing /'yō-gē-iŋ/ **verb:** **1.** An insatiably ravenous thru-hiker's superpower: turning hunger-induced charm into free food. **2.** The moral equivalent of "I'm not asking, but if you're offering . . ."

yurt /'yurt/ **noun:** **1.** A round, cozy structure, best for those who want to camp without actually camping. **2.** The mothership for social media influencers.

See also: glamping

yogi-ing

Z

zero day /ˈzir-(ˌ)ō ˈdā/ *noun:* A rest day that arrives when you're so tired that you can barely count beyond zero. For elite backpackers who thru-hike thousands of miles in a single trip, a zero day is the shimmering oasis at the end of a sweaty-and-hot slog. A zero means you don't go anywhere, you don't move camps, you don't hike a single mile. Instead, you consume some delicious calories, lollygag in the sunshine, dip your toes in an icy cold stream, and generally sit around all afternoon wondering what in the world inspired you to undertake a thru-hike in the first place.

See also: nero day

zipper /ˈzi-pər/ *noun:* The unsung hero of your camping trip. Whether it's on your hiking pants, jacket, rain shell, sleeping pad, or tent, you'd be lost without this magical metal tool that seals you inside and releases you later. Tradeoff: Zippers also devour your sleeping bag and chow down on tent flaps. You've been warned.

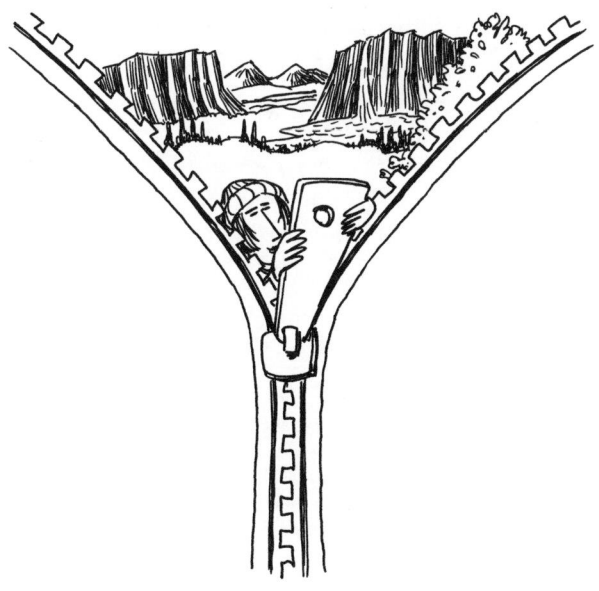